WINDRUSH
THE COMMONWEALTH
&

BY
SHALINI VALLEPUR

Passenger Opportunity To United Kingdom.

Troopship "Empire Windrush" sailing about 23rd May.
Fare — £28

BookLife
PUBLISHING

©2020
BookLife Publishing Ltd.
King's Lynn
Norfolk PE30 4LS

ISBN: 978-1-83927-092-5

Written by:
Shalini Vallepur

Edited by:
Madeline Tyler

Designed by:
Drue Rintoul

CONTENTS

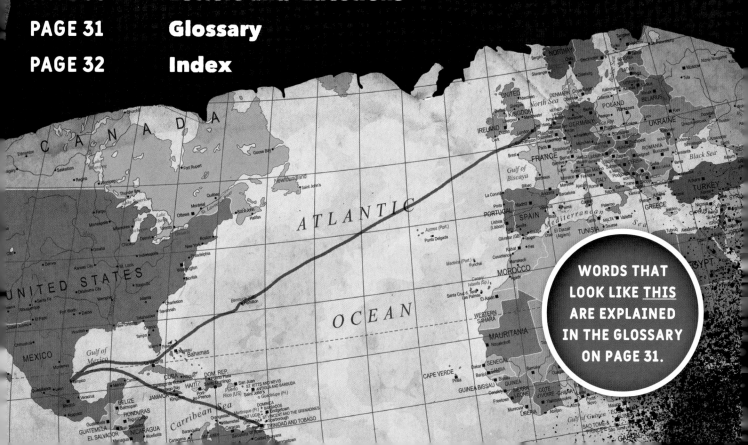

WORDS THAT LOOK LIKE <u>THIS</u> ARE EXPLAINED IN THE GLOSSARY ON PAGE 31.

THE MOVEMENT OF PEOPLE

Take a look at the world around you. How many planes take off each day? How many ships set sail? Throughout time, people have moved around the planet.

They have explored, traded and even fought with other people from across the world. All of this is possible through the movement of people.

Our world is never still. People have always wanted to explore and move around the planet and will continue to do so for years to come. Countries have borders and the sky is the limit. How does this affect the world and how is the movement of people between different countries controlled?

WHY MOVE?

People travel for lots of different reasons. Some people travel to go on holiday, and some people might travel to find a new home. There are different reasons for why people move around or leave their home country to find a new place to live.

These reasons are sometimes called push and pull factors. Think about it this way: what things might push somebody to leave their home, and what things might pull them to a new one and mean it's a better place to live?

PUSH FACTORS

- NOT ENOUGH JOBS
- PERSECUTION
- LACK OF SAFETY
- WAR
- NATURAL DISASTERS
- FAMINE

PULL FACTORS

- MORE JOB OPPORTUNITIES
- FREEDOM FROM PERSECUTION
- SAFETY AND SECURITY
- BETTER EDUCATION OPPORTUNITIES
- BETTER HEALTHCARE

WHO'S WHO?

Migration means movement. There are lots of different words that you might hear to describe the status of people who migrate. Here are a few to help you understand.

ASYLUM SEEKER: a refugee who has left their home country and has applied for safety, or asylum, in another country

EMIGRANT: a person who leaves their home country permanently, for another country

IMMIGRANT: a person who comes to live in a new country permanently, usually for work

REFUGEE: a person who has been forced to leave their home country or an asylum seeker who has been given permission to stay in another country

SETTLED: a person who lives in the UK permanently and is allowed to stay for as long as they like

THE COMMONWEALTH

Have you ever heard of the Commonwealth? The Commonwealth is currently a group of 53 countries. Although the Commonwealth is not ruled by the UK, the king or queen of the UK is the Head of the Commonwealth.

CANADA

THE UK

QUEEN ELIZABETH II

THE CARIBBEAN

QUEEN ELIZABETH II BECAME HEAD OF THE COMMONWEALTH WHEN HER FATHER KING GEORGE VI, THE PREVIOUS HEAD OF THE COMMONWEALTH, DIED IN 1952.

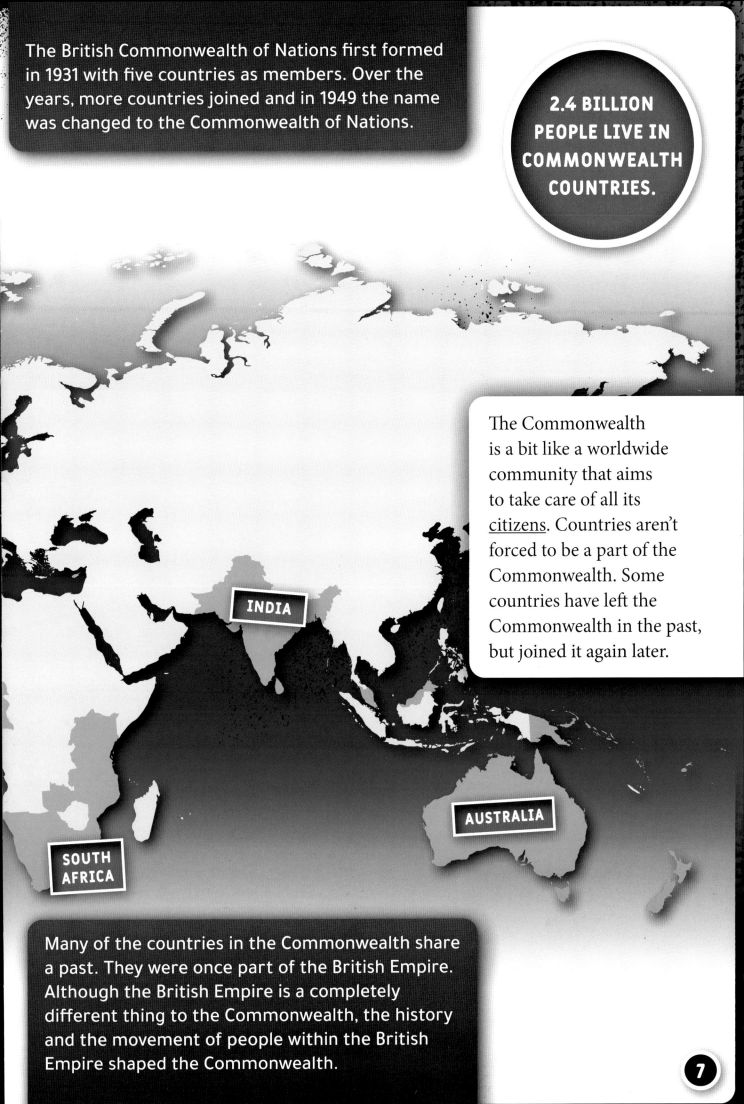

The British Commonwealth of Nations first formed in 1931 with five countries as members. Over the years, more countries joined and in 1949 the name was changed to the Commonwealth of Nations.

2.4 BILLION PEOPLE LIVE IN COMMONWEALTH COUNTRIES.

The Commonwealth is a bit like a worldwide community that aims to take care of all its citizens. Countries aren't forced to be a part of the Commonwealth. Some countries have left the Commonwealth in the past, but joined it again later.

INDIA

AUSTRALIA

SOUTH AFRICA

Many of the countries in the Commonwealth share a past. They were once part of the British Empire. Although the British Empire is a completely different thing to the Commonwealth, the history and the movement of people within the British Empire shaped the Commonwealth.

THE BRITISH EMPIRE

WHAT IS AN EMPIRE?

An empire is a group of countries or areas that are led by a ruling country and leader. Usually, the ruling country is very powerful and controls the other countries and areas by force. There have been many empires throughout history.

There is a lot of movement of people within empires. People from the ruling country usually travelled within the empire. Slavery was very common in empires of the past. People were taken and moved around empires to work as enslaved people.

THE ROMAN EMPIRE IS A FAMOUS EMPIRE FROM HISTORY. IT BEGAN IN 27 BC AND ENDED IN AD 476.

HADRIAN'S WALL WAS BUILT IN AD 128 TO CONTROL THE MOVEMENT OF PEOPLE IN ROMAN BRITAIN. IT KEPT PEOPLE OUT OF THE ROMAN EMPIRE.

THE BRITISH EMPIRE

The biggest empire in history was the British Empire. British sailors and explorers travelled around the world and reached new lands that no Europeans had been to before. Britain began to colonise different lands as early as the 1500s.

BRITAIN IS THE ISLAND THAT IS MADE UP OF ENGLAND, SCOTLAND AND WALES. THE UK IS MADE UP OF BRITAIN AND NORTHERN IRELAND, AND THE NAME WAS FIRST USED IN 1922.

AT ITS LARGEST, THE BRITISH EMPIRE COVERED AROUND ONE-QUARTER OF THE LAND ON EARTH AND RULED AROUND 400 MILLION PEOPLE.

THE NEW WORLD

Some of the new lands that Britain explored and colonised were North and South America. They began calling the Americas the 'New World', while Europe, Asia and Africa were thought of as the 'Old World'. Many Europeans were pulled to the New World because it was a chance to make money. Britain wasn't the only power with an empire – France, Spain, Portugal and the Netherlands colonised parts of the New World and had their own powerful empires.

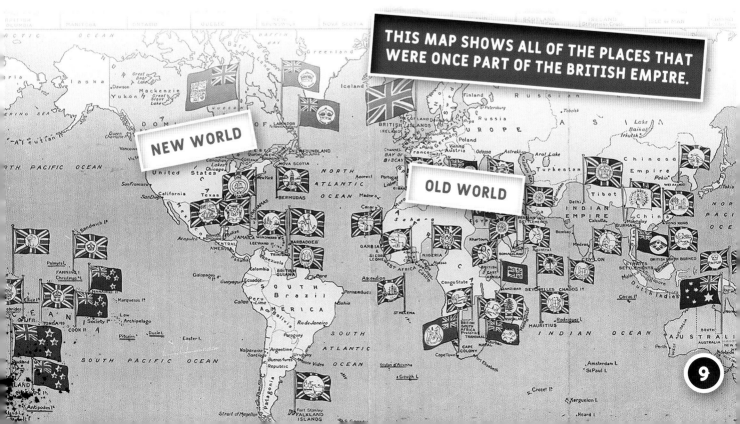

THIS MAP SHOWS ALL OF THE PLACES THAT WERE ONCE PART OF THE BRITISH EMPIRE.

NEW WORLD

OLD WORLD

MOVEMENT AROUND THE
BRITISH EMPIRE

BUYING AND SELLING

The British Empire set up companies in different areas of the world to buy and sell things. The East India Company was set up in India in 1600 so that the British Empire could take part in the spice trade across Asia. When China gave Hong Kong to the British Empire, this helped trade even more. The buying and selling of tea, coffee, sugar and cotton changed the culture and way of life in Britain as well as many other European countries.

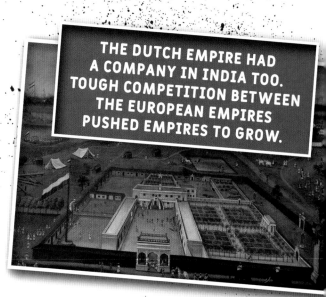

THE DUTCH EMPIRE HAD A COMPANY IN INDIA TOO. TOUGH COMPETITION BETWEEN THE EUROPEAN EMPIRES PUSHED EMPIRES TO GROW.

INDENTURED SERVANTS WERE NOT ENSLAVED PEOPLE, BUT THEY COULD BE SOLD TO DIFFERENT BUYERS JUST LIKE ENSLAVED PEOPLE.

SETTLEMENTS

Settlements were important to growing empires. Settlements, or colonies, of the British Empire were areas of land outside of Britain where people built communities. Many people were pulled to new colonies in search of jobs. New laws were made that meant more people could be sent to the colonies; instead of being punished in Britain, criminals were sent to work in the New World. Some men and women became indentured servants. Indentured servants agreed to work in the colonies for free transport to the New World.

AROUND 50,000 CRIMINALS WERE SENT TO THE NEW WORLD IN THE 1700S.

COLONISING THE CARIBBEAN

The Caribbean was colonised by Britain, Spain, the Netherlands and France. The empires used the land in the Caribbean to grow crops such as sugarcane, tobacco and rice. Along with settlements, plantations were built to grow crops. The crops were sold for a lot of money within the empires, making plantation owners very rich, and introducing new foods to people in Europe. Europeans were not the first people in the Caribbean. Indigenous people had lived there for thousands of years. When the Europeans arrived, they forced many of the indigenous people to work as enslaved people and grow their crops.

SLAVERY IN THE CARIBBEAN

Many indigenous people were killed by the Europeans, or died because of the harsh treatment and illnesses they caught from the colonisers. More workers and enslaved people were needed to grow the crops. Empires turned to the slave trade. Around 5 million enslaved African people were brought from Africa to the Caribbean to work for European empires. Around half of the enslaved African people belonged to the British Empire alone. Over time, there were more enslaved African people in the Caribbean than white Europeans. The movement of enslaved people changed the landscape of the Caribbean.

IT WAS DURING THIS TIME THAT EUROPEAN SCIENTISTS CREATED THE IDEA OF RACE. EMPIRES THEN FELT THAT THEY COULD GET AWAY WITH ENSLAVING CERTAIN PEOPLE. ENSLAVED AFRICAN PEOPLE AND OTHER PEOPLE WERE TREATED TERRIBLY BECAUSE OF THIS.

ENDING THE EMPIRE?

THE ABOLITION OF SLAVERY

In 1833, Britain <u>abolished</u> slavery in most of its colonies. Before this, many enslaved African people started <u>uprisings</u> that put a lot of pressure on the British Empire. Some previously enslaved people travelled to Britain to show how badly they had been treated. William Wilberforce was an abolitionist who saw what had happened. He began to believe that slavery was wrong. Wilberforce worked with people who used to be enslaved, as well as other abolitionists, to stop slavery. Groups such as the Pro Slavery Lobby believed that slavery was good. Eventually, slavery was abolished and around 800,000 enslaved African people in British colonies were freed.

ABOLITION GROUPS USED PICTURES LIKE THIS TO MAKE PEOPLE QUESTION SLAVERY.

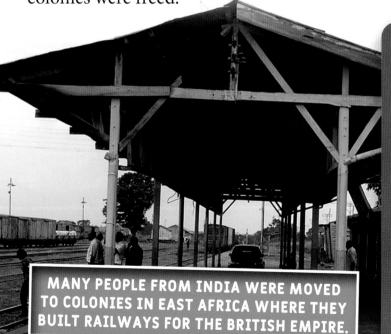

MANY PEOPLE FROM INDIA WERE MOVED TO COLONIES IN EAST AFRICA WHERE THEY BUILT RAILWAYS FOR THE BRITISH EMPIRE.

Although slavery was mostly abolished in the Caribbean, the British Empire still forced some people to work. Indentured servants from India and China were moved to places as far away as South America to work for the British Empire. They were paid very little and treated so badly that some people saw this as another form of slavery. At the time, many people were angry at how the British Empire treated its people. Many people are still angry today.

THE EMPIRE AND WORLD WAR ONE

Men and women from the British Empire were called to fight for Britain during World War One. At the start of the war in 1914, Britain's army was made up of around 700,000 people. By the end of the war in 1918, the army was made up of around 4 million people, most of whom were from British colonies.

IT IS THOUGHT THAT 1 MILLION MEN FROM WHAT IS NOW INDIA, PAKISTAN AND BANGLADESH VOLUNTEERED TO FIGHT FOR BRITAIN DURING WORLD WAR ONE.

A CHANGED WORLD

The British Empire shaped the world as we know it through the movement of people. Millions of people migrated and colonised the New and Old Worlds. Millions more were moved to new countries, whether they were enslaved people, indentured workers or criminals.

Countries with empires changed and became richer thanks to the slave trade and plantations. However, many people suffered and died because of the British Empire. Alongside the violence and destruction, new countries, cultures and ways of life were born as people moved around the world.

INTO THE COMMONWEALTH

The British Empire changed during the 20th century. While it was still known as the British Empire and there were still colonies around the world, the Commonwealth was created and more countries were gaining <u>independence</u> from British rule.

UPRISINGS AND THE FIGHT FOR INDEPENDENCE

Uprisings against the British Empire were seen throughout the colonies as more countries wanted independence from Britain. These uprisings were extremely violent and led to the deaths of thousands of people. It became too hard for Britain to control its colonies and many countries wanted more freedom after World War One. After World War One, Canada, Australia, New Zealand and South Africa became independent from Britain and became part of the British Commonwealth of Nations when it first began in 1931. The Commonwealth is a group of countries who were once part of the British Empire but who still want to be friends and work together. Other countries, such as India and those in the Caribbean, were not given independence.

THE FIGHT FOR INDEPENDENCE

Just like in World War One, Britain called upon men and women from the empire and the British Commonwealth of Nations to fight for them during World War Two. It is believed that without help from the Commonwealth and British Empire, the <u>Allies</u> would not have won World War Two. Thousands of soldiers from India fought for Britain and Britain promised to give India independence once the war was over. Britain kept this promise and granted India independence. India split to form India and Pakistan. While India left the British Empire and joined the Commonwealth, most African and Caribbean colonies were not independent until the 1960s and Hong Kong was not returned to China until 1997.

MAHATMA GANDHI FOUGHT FOR INDIA'S INDEPENDENCE FROM THE BRITISH EMPIRE.

MANY PEOPLE THINK THE BRITISH EMPIRE ONLY ENDED IN 1997.

WINNERS FROM THE 2018 COMMONWEALTH GAMES

THE COMMONWEALTH GAMES

The Commonwealth Games are a sporting event held every four years. Although the Commonwealth began in 1931, the first Commonwealth Games was actually held in 1930, but it was called the Empire Games. The Commonwealth Games is a chance for members of the Commonwealth to come together and compete in a selection of sports.

POST-WAR BRITAIN

Britain after World War Two, also known as post-war Britain, went through lots of changes. The National Health Service (NHS) was created in 1948 and the government made lots of changes to the education, transport and postal services. Although the UK was on the side that won World War Two, the independence of many countries from the British Empire meant that the UK lost much of its power in the world. On top of this, there weren't enough workers in the UK to make the government changes happen.

BOMBING DURING WORLD WAR TWO DESTROYED LARGE PARTS OF SOME UK CITIES, AND THERE WEREN'T ENOUGH WORKERS TO REBUILD.

THE BRITISH NATIONALITY ACT 1948

The government wanted to bring people from the Commonwealth to the UK in order to help the worker shortage and rebuild the UK. In 1948, the British Nationality Act was created. The act said that all people living in the United Kingdom, its colonies and the Commonwealth were to become 'British subjects' or 'Commonwealth citizens'. It also said that people could become British citizens by descent. This meant if somebody's father was a British subject or citizen, they were one too.

WORKERS IN THE UK HAD TO BUY A STAMP LIKE THIS AND PAY MONEY TO THE GOVERNMENT.

BEING A BRITISH SUBJECT

British subjects or Commonwealth citizens had freedom of movement. This meant they could travel to the UK without many <u>restrictions</u>. They could also live and work permanently in the UK if they wanted to.

WELCOME TO
THE UK

An advertisement was put into a Jamaican newspaper to pull some workers into the UK. It said there were 300 places on a ship travelling to Britain and each ticket cost £28. It is thought that the tickets were expensive to make it harder for less wealthy brown and Black people to come to the UK. However, many people in the Caribbean were pushed to the UK in search of better jobs or had been to the UK before and wanted to return.

Passenger Opportunity To United Kingdom.

Troopship "Empire Windrush" sailing about 23rd May.
Fare — £28

£28 AT THE TIME WOULD HAVE BEEN WORTH AROUND £1,000 TODAY.

HMT EMPIRE
WINDRUSH

In 1948, the HMT Empire Windrush ship set sail from the Caribbean and made its way across the Atlantic Ocean for the UK. The Windrush stopped at different countries including Trinidad, Jamaica and Cuba, which are all in the Caribbean, as well as other countries such as Mexico and Bermuda and picked up men, women and children.

IT TOOK 22 DAYS FOR THE HMT WINDRUSH TO REACH THE UK.

BERMUDA

CUBA

MEXICO

TRINIDAD

JAMAICA

TO THE MOTHERLAND

Many passengers on board were excited to reach the UK, or the 'motherland'. As many countries in the Caribbean were part of the British Empire, and the Commonwealth, they knew about the UK. Children were taught in school that the UK was the 'motherland', or the 'mother country', that had colonised and looked after their country in the past. They grew up British, even singing the British national anthem, 'God Save the King'. Many of the adults on board the Windrush knew all about Britain, even if they had never set foot there before.

BRITAIN

ON BOARD THE
WINDRUSH

There were 684 men, 257 women and 86 children on board the Windrush. Not all of the passengers were from the Caribbean. Some of the passengers on board were Polish people who were <u>displaced</u> after World War Two.

Some passengers had fought for Britain during World War Two, and were excited to return to the UK. Many of the passengers on board were skilled workers. Some were hairdressers, nurses, carpenters and there was even a <u>barrister</u> on board! Everybody was ready to rebuild the motherland.

THE WINDRUSH GENERATION

Those on board the HMT Empire Windrush were the first members of the 'Windrush generation'. Although they were not the first Black or non-European people to live in the UK, the arrival of the Windrush generation marked the start of post-war migration to the UK.

JOHN BLANKE, A MAN FROM AFRICA, PLAYED THE TRUMPET FOR HENRY VIII IN LONDON IN 1509. MANY HISTORIANS BELIEVE BLACK AND OTHER NON-EUROPEAN PEOPLE LIVED IN THE UK AS FAR BACK AS THE ROMAN EMPIRE.

BUNK BEDS WERE LINED UP IN THE AIR RAID SHELTER. SOME WINDRUSH MIGRANTS SAID THEY FELT UNWELCOME AND THAT THE SHELTER WAS CRAMPED AND NOISY. THE IDEA OF THE WELCOMING MOTHERLAND WAS SOON FORGOTTEN.

A COLD WELCOME

The Windrush landed at Tilbury Docks in Essex on the 21st of June, 1948. Some passengers on board had arranged to stay in houses in cities across the UK. There wasn't enough housing in London, so 236 migrants were sent to stay deep underground in an air raid shelter underneath Clapham South tube station while they looked for somewhere to live.

A NEW WORKFORCE

Some of the passengers of the Windrush went to work for the new government services. Nurses were employed by the NHS and other people went on to work in transport and for the postal service. Many others, however, struggled to find jobs. This surprised some of the passengers as they believed that the UK had invited them to work there.

THE TERM 'WINDRUSH GENERATION' APPLIES TO PEOPLE WHO MOVED TO THE UK FROM THE CARIBBEAN BETWEEN 1948 AND 1971.

CARIBBEAN COMMUNITIES

Many of the passengers eventually settled in Brixton and Clapham in London. The houses here were cheap and close to local job centres. These areas became the heart of the Caribbean community in London.

RESTRICTING MOVEMENT

A GROWING POPULATION

Migration to the UK from Commonwealth countries didn't stop after the HMT Empire Windrush. Thousands of Chinese, Indian and Pakistani migrants came to the UK alongside those from the Caribbean. Indian communities in Uganda moved to the UK when the Ugandan president forced all Indians to leave Uganda. Many of these Indian communities were set up by the British Empire in the past and the Indians who lived there were British. It is thought that around 470,000 people moved from Commonwealth countries to the UK between 1955 and 1962.

THE GROWING POPULATION INTRODUCED LOTS OF NEW THINGS TO THE UK, INCLUDING FOOD.

MANY OF THE WORKERS DIDN'T PLAN TO STAY FOR LONG, BUT THEY EVENTUALLY SETTLED IN THE UK.

The immigrants added to the UK workforce and boosted the UK economy. Certain businesses were able to grow. Steel and textile businesses invited workers from Pakistan and Bangladesh. These workers were ready to work during the night when other people didn't want to, which massively helped the businesses to grow.

IMMIGRATION ACTS

Despite the benefits to the economy, on the 18th of April, 1962, the Commonwealth Immigration Act was passed. This act was made to control and restrict the movement of Commonwealth citizens into the UK. The Immigration Act of 1971 made more changes to the laws. If somebody had a British passport and wanted to settle in the UK, they had to have a <u>work permit</u> and prove that one of their parents or grandparents had been born in the UK. Commonwealth citizens who were already living in the UK were given the 'right to abode' or 'indefinite leave to remain'.

WHEN SOMEONE HAS THE 'RIGHT TO ABODE' OR 'INDEFINITE LEAVE TO REMAIN', IT MEANS THEY CAN LIVE AND WORK IN THE UK FREELY, WITHOUT ANY RESTRICTION.

KEEPING COUNT

Many of the children who joined their parents in the UK after the Commonwealth Immigration Act 1962 was passed didn't have any documents of their own as they didn't need any at the time. The Home Office in the UK did not keep track of, or give documents to, the people who were given the right to abode in the UK either.

THE UK HOME OFFICE IS IN CHARGE OF IMMIGRATION TO THE UK. IT CONTROLS WHO GETS BRITISH PASSPORTS AND <u>VISAS</u>.

WHAT WENT WRONG?

Why did the UK government want to control and stop people from the Commonwealth moving to the UK when they were considered British and brought about many positive changes that helped the economy? Let's take a look at some of the reactions to the Windrush generation.

CULTURE CLASH

Although the Windrush generation were considered British, and saw themselves as being British, many white Britons did not agree. While many of the Windrush generation knew all about the motherland and grew up thinking of themselves as being British, many white Britons living in the UK knew very little about the Commonwealth or the British Empire. Groups such as the British Union Movement and the White Defence League formed. These groups wanted Caribbean people and immigrants to leave the UK. They had an idea of what it meant to be British and they didn't want what they thought of as 'British culture' to change. Some members of these groups armed themselves with weapons to attack or 'hunt' Caribbean migrants.

No Blacks
No Dogs
No Irish

LONDON 1966

DAVID PITT, A DOCTOR FROM GRENADA, WORKED HARD TO STOP RACIAL DISCRIMINATION AND BECAME THE FIRST BLACK MAN FROM THE CARIBBEAN TO SIT IN UK PARLIAMENT. HE BECAME A LORD IN 1975.

SUS LAWS AND THE COLOUR BAR

Many of the Windrush generation faced racist treatment and prejudice. Sus laws had existed in the UK since 1824. The laws allowed police to stop, search and even arrest people who looked suspicious, or people who they thought were about to commit a crime. Police used sus laws to wrongly stop and arrest Black men simply because they were Black. There were no laws to stop racial discrimination. The 'colour bar' was a form of prejudice. Black, brown and some white people were refused jobs and houses. Some couldn't go to certain churches or pubs. Some white Britons refused to work alongside Black people. Many of the Windrush generation, especially those who had fought for Britain during the war, were surprised that they were treated badly.

NOTTING HILL RACE RIOTS

In August 1958, <u>riots</u> between young white people and Black people shocked the UK. The riots are believed to have started when Raymond, a man from Jamaica, was arguing in the streets with his Swedish wife Majbritt. A crowd of white men thought that Majbritt needed help, and a fight broke out between the white men and Raymond's friends from the Caribbean. The next day, crowds of up to 400 white men charged through Notting Hill, armed and ready to attack. The police couldn't hold back the crowds, and it was only when some Jamaican men fought back that the rioting began to come to an end.

The Royal Borough of Kensington and Chelsea

NOTTING HILL GATE, W.11.

EVENTS SUCH AS THE CARIBBEAN CARNIVAL AND NOTTING HILL CARNIVAL WERE MADE TO HELP BRING PEOPLE TOGETHER. FIND OUT MORE ON PAGE 26.

KELSO COCHRANE

In May, 1959, Kelso Cochrane was attacked and killed by a group of young white men while walking home. Many people were shocked by the attack, especially as the men were never caught. Some believed that the police weren't looking into the death properly because Cochrane was Black. <u>Protests</u> were held, demanding changes be made to the laws.

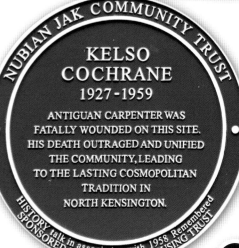

NUBIAN JAK COMMUNITY TRUST

KELSO COCHRANE
1927-1959
ANTIGUAN CARPENTER WAS FATALLY WOUNDED ON THIS SITE. HIS DEATH OUTRAGED AND UNIFIED THE COMMUNITY, LEADING TO THE LASTING COSMOPOLITAN TRADITION IN NORTH KENSINGTON.

HISTORY talk in association with 1958 Remembered SPONSORED BY KENSINGTON HOUSING TRUST

THE IMPACT OF THE WINDRUSH GENERATION

The movement of people can often introduce new cultures to an area. Sometimes people get angry about this, but most of the time, different cultures and ways of life can exist together. This is called multiculturalism. The Windrush generation and others who moved to the UK brought lots of things that we still enjoy today. From music and art to food and festivals, different cultures have shaped the UK into what it is today.

PEOPLE FROM DIFFERENT BACKGROUNDS VISIT BRIXTON TO ENJOY THE MUSIC AND FOOD.

CARIBBEAN COSTUMES, MUSIC AND FOOD ARE CELEBRATED AT THE CARNIVAL.

NOTTING HILL CARNIVAL

Notting Hill Carnival is an event that happens every year in London. It was started in 1966 by Rhaune Laslett-O'Brien. She wanted to help the relationships between white and Black people in Notting Hill. Laslett-O'Brien was inspired by Claudia Jones who ran a similar carnival called the Caribbean Carnival, held every year for six years, starting in 1959. Laslett-O'Brien and Jones both fought for the rights of the Windrush generation. In order to bring people together, Jones started a carnival. Notting Hill Carnival was inspired by Caribbean culture and still brings people together today.

THE WINDRUSH SCANDAL

In 2018, thousands of British citizens from the Windrush generation had their status questioned by the Home Office. The Home Office had not kept a record of people who had been allowed to remain, and many members of the Windrush generation had no way to prove they were in the UK legally. This became known as the Windrush scandal. How did this happen and what effect did it have?

THE HOSTILE ENVIRONMENT POLICY

In 2012, the Home Office introduced the hostile environment policy. The policy made it harder for people without the right to abode to stay in the UK. Hospitals, banks and even <u>landlords</u> were able to ask people to prove their identity and status with documents before treating or serving them. Many thought that this new policy would lead to racial discrimination because non-white people were more likely to have their status questioned.

Thousands of people from the Windrush generation had their status questioned because of the hostile environment policy, even though they were living in the UK legally, and had been for years. Those who came to the UK as children before the Immigration Act 1971 did not have the documents needed to prove their status as they were not given any when they arrived in the UK and the Home Office didn't keep a record.

THE DAMAGE

Many people were affected by the Windrush scandal. Some people lost their jobs or were made homeless because they couldn't prove their status when asked. Some people were held in immigration <u>detention centres</u>. They had to wait for the Home Office to decide whether they were allowed to stay in the UK or not. British citizens who had lived and worked in the country for years were suddenly treated as though they were in the country illegally.

IMMIGRATION DETENTION CENTRES ARE NOT PRISONS, BUT SOME PEOPLE HAVE SAID IT FEELS LIKE ONE INSIDE.

In some cases, people stopped having access to free hospital services. Some people couldn't afford treatment or were so afraid of being questioned or <u>deported</u> that they didn't go to the hospital when they needed to. Dexter Bristol moved to the UK in 1968 when he was eight years old. He died in 2018, shortly after being told that he was not a British citizen. He lost his job and became extremely stressed and depressed. Some doctors think that the stress caused by the Windrush scandal could have led to his death.

FIGHT BRITAIN'S RACIST IMMIGRATION LAWS!
No deportations!
FIGHT RACISM! FIGHT IMPERIALISM!

IN 2018, IT WAS ANNOUNCED THAT 83 BRITISH CITIZENS HAD BEEN WRONGFULLY DEPORTED FROM THE UK.

A FAILED POLICY

The hostile environment policy didn't take into account the past. Some people, and even some MPs, believed that the policy was racist. It didn't take into account the history of the British Empire or the Commonwealth and the policies and laws that controlled the movement of people in the past.

BRITISH IDENTITY

The Windrush scandal brought up many questions about identity and being British. What does it mean to be British and what makes somebody British? Theresa May, who was the British prime minister at the time, apologised to those affected by the Windrush scandal and for all the stress and hurt that the Home Office caused. She also claimed that the UK government would help to support those who had lost their jobs and money because of the scandal.

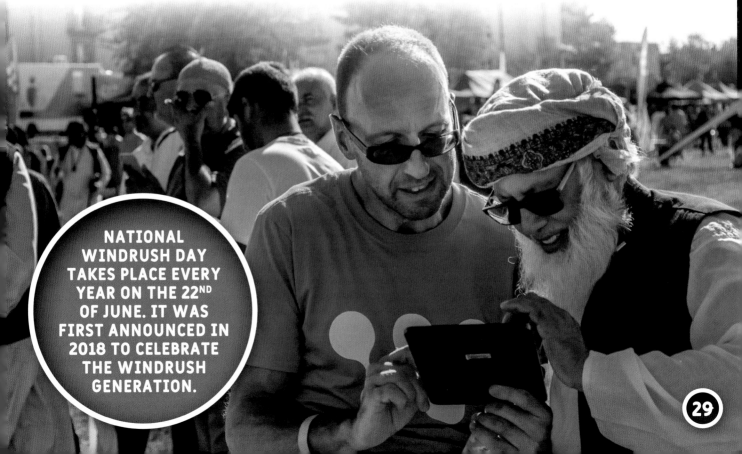

NATIONAL WINDRUSH DAY TAKES PLACE EVERY YEAR ON THE 22ND OF JUNE. IT WAS FIRST ANNOUNCED IN 2018 TO CELEBRATE THE WINDRUSH GENERATION.

LETTERS AND QUESTIONS

LETTERS HOME

Imagine you are on a crowded ship moving to a new country. You have never been there before but you have heard lots of good things about it. Write a letter to your family back home, telling them how you feel and what you are excited for.

Imagine you have arrived at your new home. Things are not how you expected. How do you feel about it? Write a letter to your family back home explaining how you feel and what you are doing.

THINGS TO THINK ABOUT

Sometimes it can be tricky to understand what's happening in the world. It's important to talk to lots of different people about the world. You can learn a lot by sharing your story and listening to other people's stories.

Try answering the following questions with your family and friends. You might learn something new about somebody!

- Have you ever moved school, house or country? How did you feel about moving?
- How would you welcome a new neighbour that moved from far away?
- How would you feel if you were made to move away from your home?
- How would you feel if you moved somewhere new and people stopped you from doing the things you like?

IF ASKING OTHER PEOPLE THESE QUESTIONS SOUNDS A BIT SCARY, YOU COULD TRY ASKING YOURSELF SOME OF THEM INSTEAD. IT MAY HELP YOU TO UNDERSTAND YOUR OWN FEELINGS AND YOU MAY EVEN LEARN SOMETHING NEW ABOUT YOURSELF!

GLOSSARY

abolished when something has been stopped

Allies a group of countries, including Great Britain, the US, China, the Soviet Union and France, that were on the same side during World War Two

arrest when police stop and take somebody away for breaking the law

asylum protection given to somebody by a state or government

barrister a type of lawyer

citizens people belonging to a certain place who therefore have certain rights in that place

colonise when people move to a new land and take control of the area and people

deported when somebody has been made to leave the country they emigrated to

detention centres places where people are held while waiting for a government to make decisions about their future

displaced when somebody has been forced to leave their home

economy the way trade and money is made and controlled by a country or region

famine when large numbers of people do not have enough food

government the group of people with the power to run a country and decide its laws

independence when an area or country is not ruled by another country and has control of itself

indigenous belonging to, or coming from, a certain area

landlords people who rent houses and properties out to other people

MPs members of Parliament – people who have been chosen to help run a country

natural disasters natural events, such as earthquakes or floods, that cause serious damage and loss of life

Parliament in the UK, the group of people who run the country

permanently lasting forever

persecution cruel or unfair treatment based on religion, political beliefs, where a person is from or what they look like

plantations large farms that are used to grow crops

prejudice opinions, judgements or beliefs that are formed without thinking about facts

protests actions that show disagreement with something

race the incorrect belief system created by European scientists that said people should be grouped together based on what they look like or where they come from and that certain groups should be treated badly compared to others

racial discrimination the unfair treatment of people based on what they look like or the culture they come from

restrictions limits or things that are put in place to stop something happening

riots times when large groups of people behave in violent and uncontrolled ways

slave trade the buying and selling of enslaved people

slavery to do with owning other people, called enslaved people, who have no freedom

status a person's position and situation at a particular time, to do with moving to new countries

suspicious when someone looks like they are doing something they shouldn't be doing

tobacco a plant with leaves that are smoked or chewed

uprisings when groups of people stand up for themselves, sometimes using violence

visas when permissions have been given for a person to visit a certain country or stay for a certain amount of time

work permit a document that gives a person permission to work in a certain country

INDEX